MW01115209

UTAH

A PICTURE MEMORY

Text
Bill Harris

Captions
Nicola Dent

Design
Teddy Hartshorn

Photography
Colour Library Books Ltd.
Tom Till

Editorial
David Gibbon

Production
Ruth Arthur
Sally Connolly
Neil Randles

Director of Production
Gerald Hughes

CLB 2875
© 1990 Colour Library Books Ltd., Godalming, Surrey, England.
All rights reserved.
This 1994 edition is published by Crescent Books,
distributed by Random House Value Publishing Inc.,
40 Engelhard Avenue, Avenel, New Jersey 07001.
Color separations by Scantrans Pte Ltd., Singapore.
Printed and bound in Singapore.
ISBN 0 517 07262 9
8 7 6 5 4 3 2

UTAH

A PICTURE MEMORY

CRESCENT BOOKS
NEW YORK • AVENEL, NEW JERSEY

In 1776, when Europeans on America's East Coast were making plans to unite their colonies into a nation, Spanish explorers in the West were looking for ways to join their colonies, too. The Spanish empire was already established in New Mexico and had recently pushed into California, and it was important to map a route across the mountains to get from one to the other. Their search led them to Utah Lake, whose valley, one of them noted, was "the most pleasing, beautiful and fertile site in all New Spain." They turned south again at that point and headed back to Santa Fe, but after writing a glowing report on its abundance of wildlife, pasturage and water, and noting that the valley could support several large settlements, the expedition's leader, Father Silvestre Velez de Escalante, also revealed that there was an even larger lake just to the north. He said that its waters were "noxious and extremely salty," but he based the opinion on an Indian statement that touching the water made their skin itch, and never went to see for himself. Escalante noted that the natives were friendly, but the decision-makers in Mexico City had seen quite enough of hostile Plains Indians, and when the padre said that the Utes he met rarely ventured north because the Comanche considered the bison herds their private property, they decided it was best to leave Utah to the Indians.

It was a kind of no-man's land in the years that followed. The Indians eked out a meager living there and settlers bound for California were more than willing to pay them tribute to be allowed to get beyond the salt flats and rugged mountains. Mountain men who had trapped out the beaver further north began using it for their annual rendezvous, and the Salt Lake valley became the center of the Rocky Mountain fur trade. Although officially part of New Spain, it began to take on a decidedly American accent, and when the trapper Jedediah Smith arrived there for the June Rendezvous in 1827, he wrote that the lake "excited in me those feelings known to the traveler who, after long and perilous journeying, comes again in view of his home."

Although many of them would echo his feelings two decades later, almost no one back East would have understood what he was talking about at the time, least of all young Joseph Smith of Palmyra, New York.

He would begin to understand three months later, on September 21, 1827, when he received golden plates containing the Book of Mormon. Along with the Book, a record of the settlement of North America by Israelites who, according to its revelations, became the ancestors of the American Indian tribes, Smith also received a mandate to establish a New Jerusalem. He never knew it would be planted on the shores of the Great Salt Lake, in a place that would become known as Utah.

When the Book of Mormon was published in 1830, Americans were banding together to oppose everything they considered foreign. In their quest for purity, Catholics were scorned, Freemasons vilified and immigrants treated as untouchables. The nativists found a new enemy in the Church of Jesus Christ of Latter-Day Saints and, like other organizations that didn't seem to square with what they considered the American Way, there was a hue and cry to deny the Mormons such basic American rights as free speech and freedom of religion. It was soon obvious to Smith and his followers that if they were to establish the New Jerusalem they would have to go west, beyond the reach of the mobs who routinely reached for their guns at the very mention of the word Mormon.

Their first stop was Kirtland, Ohio, but within six months they established another settlement in Missouri, which the Book of Mormon said had been the original site of the Garden of Eden and predicted would be the location of the most important city in the Western Hemisphere. Kansas City would eventually rise there, but without the Mormons. The Missourians drove them out, and Joseph Smith led the Saints to the relative safety of the east bank of the Mississippi in Illinois. When they arrived in the little town of Commerce, it was at the edge of a fever-ridden swamp with no hope for any kind of future, but in five years the Mormons transformed it into a city they called Nauvoo that was not only the biggest in Illinois, with a population of 20,000, but was also the grandest city anywhere on the river.

Nauvoo operated as a city-state, with Joseph Smith not only as its spiritual leader but its political force, too. He became powerful in the Illinois state government, and by 1844 he announced that he was a candidate for the office of President of the United States. He had already built a strong missionary organization that was gathering converts in Europe as well as America, and all of them were eager to turn their talents to the political arena as well. But politics and religion are a volatile combination on the American scene, and the people of Illinois, who had welcomed the Mormons into their midst, soon became as hostile as the Missourians had been.

The end of Nauvoo began when Joseph ordered his militia to destroy the presses of a newspaper that opposed him. He was arrested and shot by an anti-Mormon mob, but neither the city nor the movement he built died with him. The state revoked Nauvoo's charter, but work continued on the half-finished temple and new converts kept pouring in. It wasn't until eighteen months after Smith's death that Brigham Young, the President of the Quorum of the Twelve Apostles, began sending advance parties to find "some good valley in the neighborhood of the Rocky Mountains," where the New Jerusalem could be established.

The first of them left Nauvoo on February 4, 1846, and seven months later the last of the Mormons were driven out. But no one was sure where they were going, and it wasn't until the following summer that the Great Salt Lake Valley was revealed to them as the site of the New Jerusalem. According to Mormon tradition, Brigham Young had seen the valley in a vision back in Nauvoo, but it's likely that he had considered other places as well. Many of his followers believed their destination was California and, in fact, a shipload of Saints sailed from New York on their way to San Francisco the same day the first contingent marched west from Nauvoo. Brigham was worried that the Mexican War, which began that spring, would bring the Southern Rocky Mountains under American control and bring them the same grief they had found in Missouri and Illinois, and some of his advisors were suggesting that they might join the British in Oregon. But one thing everyone agreed about was that their destiny was in the west, and every bright sunset was a reminder of the pillar of fire that led the children of Israel to the Promised Land.

The first wagon train had the responsibility not only of finding their unknown destination but also of planting camps along the way to help ease the trip for those who would follow them, and when a scouting party led by Orson Pratt and Erastus Snow entered the Salt Lake Valley on July 21, 1847, they didn't know that they hadn't found just another way station. But their first view of the valley cradled in snow-covered mountains was easily the most beautiful sight they had seen in their thousand-mile march from the winter camp on the Missouri River. By the time the main party, led by Brigham Young, arrived three days later, the scouts had explored the valley and had plowed three acres, irrigating it with water from a dammed-up creek. They were making plans to move on in search of the next camp site, but their leader told them it wouldn't be necessary. "This is the place," he said.

In addition to drawing up plans for the new City of Zion at the southeast corner of the Great Salt Lake, Brigham Young gave his people a set of laws that said land couldn't be bought or sold, but would be apportioned among church members whose tenure depended on how they took care of it. The decree had a corollary that all timber and water in the area belonged to the community for the benefit of all. But the only other law was the moral code of the church itself, more than enough to make the colony thrive and the desert bloom.

But although one of them wrote that "All is quiet ... no elections, no police reports, no murders, no wars in our little world," they still needed to deal with the world outside, and in 1848 they sent a proposal to Washington to create a Federal Territory that would include all of present-day Utah and Nevada as well as parts of Arizona, New Mexico, Wyoming, Idaho and Oregon. Its name, they said, would be "Deseret," a word the Book of Mormon said meant "honey bee," a symbol of abundance as well as of industry. At the time, Congress was embroiled in debate over dividing the spoils of the Mexican War into pro- and anti-slavery states, and after a year of discussion and compromise they reduced the size of the Mormon claim. In 1850 they approved its territorial status but refused to accept the name Deseret and substituted Utah, in honor of the local Indian tribe.

While the debate was raging back East, gold was discovered further west, and the Mormon settlement became an oasis for California-bound prospectors, who were willing to swap tools and clothing for food.

But few of them were able to convince any of the Saints to follow them. Brigham Young had told them that "gold is for paving streets," and convinced them that their job was to stay home and make their fields green. While nearly everyone in America was dreaming of getting rich in California, the Mormons, who were more than half-way there, stayed where they were, quietly building their kingdom in Utah.

The U.S. Government didn't have much use for a kingdom, and when officials arrived from Washington to take charge in 1851, it became obvious that they were going to have a problem with Brigham Young and the Latter-Day Saints. After a few months, they headed back for Washington with an official report that it would be "very inconvenient" for Americans to settle in the Utah Territory because "polygamy monopolizes all the women." The issue of plural wives had been a lightning rod for opponents of Mormonism from the very beginning, but although some church leaders had adopted the practice it wasn't a part of church doctrine until a year later, when a special conference was convened in Salt Lake City. Some said it was a thumbing of the Mormon nose in the direction of Washington, but the tradition actually stemmed from a revelation made by Joseph Smith in 1843, to the effect that a man's wives and children added to his glory in heaven, as well as to their own.

But except to outsiders, who the Mormons characterized as "Gentiles," polygamy was very much a side issue. Only a small percentage engaged in it and everyone in Utah had other things on their mind. Chief among them was a population explosion. When the Federal officials arrived in 1851, Brigham Young reported that there were 11,380 people in the Territory. Five years later there were 76,000, and the combination of grasshopper infestations of their farms and the increased need for food was cause for alarm. The Saints met the problem with a return to their roots and a plan to bring them more mouths to feed. After reaffirming their faith, they issued a call to poor Mormons in England to come to Zion on foot "with handcarts and wheelbarrows," and thus began one of the most incredible migrations in the history of mankind.

The first of them left Iowa City in 1856. There were about five hundred of them, mostly women and children, and fully ten percent were over the age of fifty. None of them had ever slept outdoors before, except possibly on the streets of cities, and none had ever seen a wilderness, let alone learned how to survive in one. The church financed their journey from England to the Iowa River, but for the last thousand miles they were on their own.

The procession included supply wagons, but the emigrants themselves were forced to walk, pushing handcarts, each loaded with an average of five hundred pounds of supplies in addition to their worldly goods. The trek began on June 9 and ended at Salt Lake City on September 26. Twenty-one of them, mostly children, were buried along the trail. Another contingent arrived a few days later, and the experiment was hailed as an unqualified success. But they didn't know there were other handcart pioneers out there on the prairie.

More than fifteen hundred people had arrived in Iowa City in July and were outfitted with hastily-made carts and sent on their way. Their guides knew that there would be snow in the mountains before they reached them, and they suggested creating a winter camp, but were outvoted by their zealous charges, who were convinced that God would see them through. He did, but not without testing their faith and their endurance. The first casualties were the handcarts themselves. They had been made of green wood and began to fall apart on the dry plains. At one point a herd of buffalo stampeded their cattle and oxen, leaving them with no way to haul their supply wagons. Trading posts along the trail were generally out of supplies and, as the weather grew colder, the going got tougher. Then it started to snow. They were still three hundred miles from the Great Salt Lake and their supplies were gone. In the meantime, word of their plight had reached Brigham Young, who called for volunteers to find them. The rescuers faced the same problems as the emigrants and were stopped in their tracks by a heavy snowstorm, but one of the handcart guides found their camp and reported that his charges were twenty-five miles away. It was obvious that if help didn't reach them right away, they would all die. The first group was reached in a day, but there were more of them further east and scouts headed for them through the knee-deep snow. Without supplies to offer, all they could do was encourage them to keep moving and then move on themselves to find the others. Within a few days everyone was moving again, toward supply wagons sent out from Salt Lake City. More than two-hundred of the pioneers died crossing the mountains and almost none survived without frostbite.

In spite of the experience, there would be other handcart companies bringing thousands more into Utah before the Mormons established a sophisticated system of wagon trains to bring even more home to Zion. But the prejudice in the outside world was coming to a head. In the 1856 national election, the Republican platform characterized polygamy, along with slavery, as twin evils, and the Democrats claimed that Mormonism was the greatest evil of all. Republican James Buchanan won the election and began his administration by replacing Brigham Young with a non-Mormon as Utah's territorial governor. Brigham answered by declaring martial law and calling out the militia. The president responded by ordering troops to march on Utah, but Mormon "guerillas" managed to delay them by driving off livestock and cutting their supply lines. The war never materialized, and after all the population north of the Utah Valley, including Salt Lake City, was evacuated to the south, Buchanan backed down. The army was finally withdrawn to fight in the Civil War.

The war had been predicted by Joseph Smith nearly thirty years earlier, and most Mormons believed that the collapse of the Union was the vehicle that would establish their kingdom. They refused to abandon the Union themselves, but resurrected the State of Deseret, which lasted another nine years as the shadow of a dream. But in the meantime the postwar migration of westward-bound Americans brought a flood of Gentiles into the territory, and the trans-continental railroad that crossed it ended the isolation that had allowed the Mormon dream to flourish.

But Utah still wasn't a state by any means. The Federal Government wouldn't appropriate money for it, nor grant any land titles. Everyone in Utah was technically a squatter. The real issue was Mormon authority, but polygamy was the buzz word, and the power of the federal courts was brought to bear against the practice, even though it wasn't illegal. The harassment went on until 1890, when the church officially advised its members to stop plural marriages. In return for the gesture the government pardoned polygamists and restored the civil rights it had taken away. The Utahans responded by drafting a constitution that made polygamy illegal and added a clause giving women the right to vote, a bold step at the time, and in 1896 Utah was welcomed into the Union as the 45th state.

The Mormon saga was probably the greatest success story of all the social experiments that created America. But if the Saints made the desert bloom, it was the Centiles who exploited the resources under it. Brigham Young had discouraged his people from digging for gold and silver but, with the coming of the railroad, outsiders began finding coal and copper and other minerals and founded industries that attracted even more non-Mormons. By 1890 the Mormon population of Salt Lake City had dropped to fifty percent, and the wealth from mining was fueling a growth that even its far-sighted founders never dreamed of. But if the Gentiles they hoped to leave behind followed them to the Promised Land, the Mormon spirit still pervades the atmosphere in Utah, and the beehive symbol the pioneers carried across the country is as appropriate as ever.

Salt Lake City's gracious Utah State Capitol (facing page), built in 1915, commands a fine position on Capitol Hill overlooking Temple Square and Salt Lake Valley. Designed by Utah architect Richard Kletting, this imposing, Corinthian-style building is constructed of local granite and marble, and features an impressive copper-clad dome.

Within the High Uintas Wilderness, aptly named Red Castle Peak looms behind the swift-flowing Smith Fork River (below) and beyond tranquil Lower Red Castle Lake (overleaf). Facing page: contrasting views of the Green River as it winds through snow-covered Red Canyon (top) in Flaming Gorge National Recreational Area and Whirlpool Canyon (bottom) in Dinosaur National Monument.

Rich fall colors and the brilliant red and orange of Indian paintbrush, often known as "prairie fire," decorate Mount Timpanogos Wilderness (top left and below), Albion Basin (above and bottom left) in Wasatch National Forest, and Spanish Fork Canyon (facing page). Left: the Wasatch Mountains seen beyond covered wagons on Mormon Trail, Pioneer Trail State Park, a route named for the early travelers who first explored the area. Overleaf: Timponeke Peak.

Capital of Utah, Salt Lake City (facing page bottom) is located on the southeastern shores of Great Salt Lake (bottom left and facing page top), at the foot of the Wasatch Mountains. This impressive city boasts the splendid Utah State Capitol (top left) and the striking, six-spired Mormon Temple (above). Left: the locomotive Jupiter *preserved at Golden Spike National Historic Site, where eastern and western railway tracks were joined in 1869. Below: prickly pear cacti at Promontory Point.*

Crowned by the towering spires of the Mormon Tabernacle (above), the church that is home to the famed Mormon Tabernacle Choir (below right), Salt Lake City (facing page bottom) contains a number of splendid buildings constructed in a variety of architectural styles. Among these are the ornate Richardsonian Romanesque Salt Lake City and County Building (facing page top), which was modeled on London's City Hall, the French Renaissance-style Governor's Mansion or Thomas Kearns House (right), and the grand McCune Mansion (below), constructed from imported tiles, mahogany and oak. Above right: the Eagle Gate, with the LDS Church Office Building beyond.

Arches National Park is renowned for its concentration of natural stone arches, windows and spires. Delicate Arch (center right), with the magnificent La Sal Mountains beyond, is one of the most spectacular of the park's features. And in the Windows section Turret Arch (below) and North and South windows (overleaf) are further testimony to the erosive power of the elements. Right and bottom right: old pioneer cabins at San Rafael Swell.

Millions of years of wind and water erosion have shaped the ever-changing landscape of Arches National Park. Among the area's many strange rock formations and dramatic colorings are Double Arch (facing page top), the sandstone fins of Upper Fiery Furnace (above), Turret Arch framed by North Window (right), and South Window (top right and below). Bottom right: Garden of Eden, and (facing page bottom) the orange sandstone of South Park Avenue.

The beautiful La Sal Mountains form a fine backdrop to Colorado River Canyon (below) and to this field of red globemallows (facing page top), a rare bloom that appears after abundant rains. Facing page bottom: a colorful orchard near Moab, in Lower Spanish Valley. Overleaf: Dead Horse Point State Park – named after wild horses that perished after being herded to the area – affords spectacular views over the red rock countryside of the Colorado Plateau and River.

Known for its wide variety of color and form, Canyonlands National Park attracts many visitors. Of particular renown are the carved shapes in the Needles district (facing page top, top right and below), and the remarkable vistas seen from Grand View Point (bottom right), at the tip of the mesa known as Island in the Sky. Other attractions include Angel Arch (above), the Wooden Shoe (right), and the magical view of Washerwoman Arch and the La Sal Mountains (overleaf).

Human figures illustrate the enormity of Squaw Flat (left), and of the entrance to Joint Trail (below), leading to Chesler Park – both features of the Needles district of Canyonlands (these pages). The view from the Colorado River Lookout (center left) gives an elevated overlook across the mighty Colorado River. Overleaf: ancient ruins discovered under the arches provide some evidence that the Anasazi Indians once hunted and farmed the land that is now preserved as a national park.

Valley of the Gods State Park (left), Monument Valley Tribal Park (below), and San Juan Goosenecks State Preserve (overleaf), are among Utah's many beautiful and varied recreational areas. And two of the state's fascinating national monuments are Natural Bridges, home to impressive Owachomo Bridge (center left), and Hovenweep, with its fascinating collection of well-preserved Anasazi ruins, crowned by Hovenweep Castle (bottom left).

Made up of a series of domes that encompass the Waterpocket Fold, Capitol Reef National Park was named after the largest of these, which was considered to resemble the dome of the U.S. Capitol. The Narrows (right), in mighty Capitol Gorge (center and bottom right), and sweeping arches that include Cassidy Arch (below), are well-known sights found in this splendid park. Despite being larger than Utah's Bryce and Zion national parks put together, Capital Reef is still little known to tourists.

The Castle (previous page and above), Eph Hanks Tower (top right), and imposing Egyptian Temple (right) are some of the fantastic formations that abound in Capitol Reef National Park. Facing page: Cathedral Valley (top) and Chimney Rock (bottom). Below: the well-preserved log schoolhouse at Fruita, a Mormon community whose orchards (bottom right) still flourish today. Overleaf: Glen Canyon National Recreation Area, with Navajo Mountain beyond.

Bryce Canyon National Park, with its wide range of geological wonders, is a magical place to visit. Tinted pinnacles and slender spires, sculpted by ice and wind, can be seen along Fairyland Trail (top left and below), at Bryce Point (facing page top) and at Sunrise Point (facing page bottom). A stunning panoramic view of Bryce Canyon (bottom left) gives some idea of the vastness of the area, and Paria View (left and above) is another lookout affording awe-inspiring vistas.

53

Designated a national park in 1928, Bryce Canyon was named after Ebenezer Bryce, an early Mormon settler. Different views of its eroded and brilliantly colored rocks are to be had from Fairyland Trail (above), around Queen's Garden Trail (top right, right and below), Agua Canyon (facing page top), and looking down on Navajo Loop from Sunset Point (facing page bottom). Bottom right: the remarkable structure known as Balanced Rock.

Hikers on Queen's Garden Trail (below) show the tremendous scale of the marvelously sculpted formations in Bryce Canyon National Park (these pages). Paria View (right) commands fine panoramic views of the rugged landscape, while Inspiration Point (overleaf) looks across the intricate spires and pinnacles that have caused the park to be likened to a "Gothic City." Another spectacular feature of the area is Natural Bridge (center right), the central part of which has been eroded leaving a 50-foot-wide hole.

Zion (these pages), established in 1919, is one of the country's oldest national parks. Located midway in the "Grand Stairway" between Bryce Canyon and Grand Canyon national parks, it surrounds the dramatically sculpted Zion Canyon (facing page bottom), a deep, multicolored gorge carved by the Virgin River. Facing page top: the dominating formation known as the East Temple, and (below) gleaming pools found in a grotto along the West Fork of the Virgin River.

Described as the "Yosemite of the desert," Zion is a national park of great natural beauty. Its many imposing red rock formations include Great White Throne and Temple of Sinawava (left), the Sentinel (facing page top), and the Watchman (facing page bottom), whose sheer face contrasts with delicate apricot blossom (bottom left). A waterfall (above) along the Virgin River, and sunset views of Bear Cedar City (top left) and Cedar Breaks National Monument (overleaf), are further examples of the area's appeal.